DRAW make CREATE

APT8 KIDS

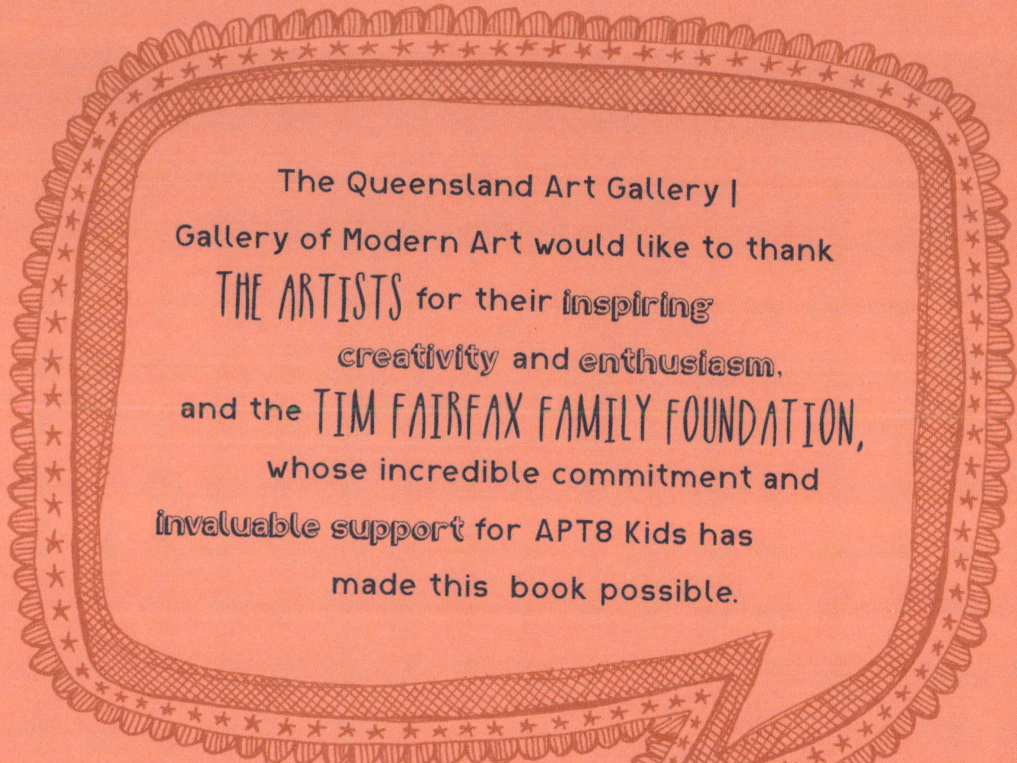
The Queensland Art Gallery | Gallery of Modern Art would like to thank THE ARTISTS for their inspiring creativity and enthusiasm, and the TIM FAIRFAX FAMILY FOUNDATION, whose incredible commitment and invaluable support for APT8 Kids has made this book possible.

THANK YOU

THIS BOOK BELONGS TO

WHAT'S
INSIDE

When I was a child I was very shy, and quiet. I LOVED to draw, read, write, make funny sculptures and secret rooms... and I LOVED to dance (I still do!).

ANGELA TIATIA

Aotearoa New Zealand/ Australia

My favourite thing about being an ARTIST is that I get to think up lots of interesting questions and while I try to find answers I get to meet lots of FUN PEOPLE.

My favourite material to work with is my IMAGINATION, In my mind anything is possible.

Self-portrait 2015
Courtesy: The artist and Alcaston Gallery, Melbourne

Heels (from 'An Inventory of Gestures' series) (still) 2014
Collection: Queensland Art Gallery

Creativity is contagious. Pass it on. Albert Einstein

Our IMAGINATION is such a powerful tool for drawing and making art. I am constantly day dreaming and drawing. THESE DRAWING EXERCISES are about making thoughts visible, the unseen seen. There is no such thing as a MISTAKE! Be free, be wild, have fun, laugh and share your drawings with others. LET'S DRAW!

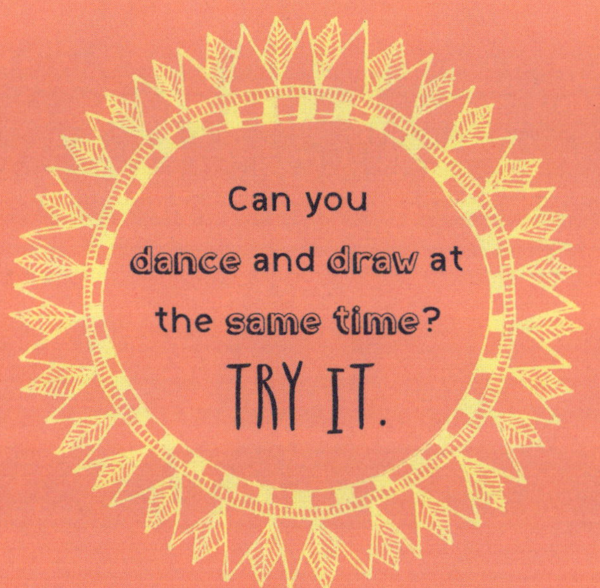

To draw, you must close your eyes and sing. Pablo Picasso

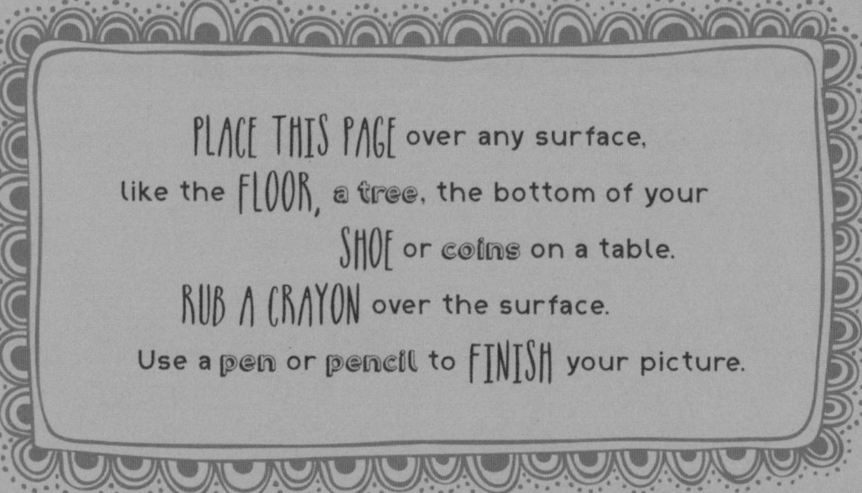

We must use time creatively. Martin Luther King, Jr.

You have to imagine it possible before you can see something. Rita Dove

Breathe in. Breathe out.

Do this again, but this time IMAGINE A WORLD

that exists within your breath

that no-one else can see but you. Draw this world.

Everything has beauty, but not everyone sees it. Confucius

I dwell in possibility. Emily Dickinson

पुष्पाकुमारी

What I LOVE about being an ARTIST is that I can draw on paper what I SEE in my imagination.

PUSHPA KUMARI

India

I am inspired by my GRANDMOTHER who was a renowned folk artist, and also by the beauty of my HOMELAND with its wonderful thatched homes, lush fields and fruit-laden trees.

Myself in Madhubani Style 2015
Courtesy: The artist

Prem jalkida (The intoxication of love and attraction) 2015
Proposed for the Queensland Art Gallery Collection

Hello FRIENDS.

I would LOVE to share with you the fun I had as a child growing up in a tiny village in Bihar, India. There was no TV, internet or video games in those days. We were always out IN THE SUN enjoying Mother Nature's bounty.

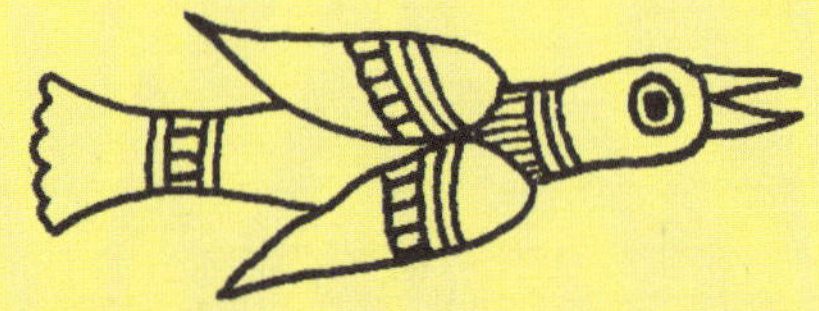

FRIENDS would get together and go fishing, fly kites and pluck mangoes from the trees (I LOVE YUMMY mangoes... do you ?). Often I would sit with my grandmother who taught me how to DRAW and COLOUR.

I have drawn some DIFFERENT borders in the Madhubani style so you can learn how to draw these too.

I have SKETCHED some scenes from my childhood for you to fill up with COLOUR.

पुष्पा कुमारी

पुष्पा कुमारी

पुष्पा कुमारी

पुष्पा कुमारी

Create your own patterned border and draw a PICTURE OF YOU doing something you enjoy.

人
土
金
水
木

I use a CHINESE brush and ink for drawing. Sometimes I make my OWN INK by grinding an ink stick with a little water.

My FAVOURITE thing about being an artist is waking up and MAKING things or pictures with my hands all day long, then going to sleep and dreaming, and DOING IT ALL again the next day.

SHARON CHIN

Malaysia

I LOVE every stick and stone, every bug and squirrel in the PLACE I live. I love the trees and the road, the neighbours and the SEA nearby.

Self-portrait in Fire (火), *Earth* (土), *Metal* (金), *Water* (水) *and Wood* (木) 2015
Courtesy: The artist

Mandi Bunga/Flower Bath 2013
Courtesy: The artist

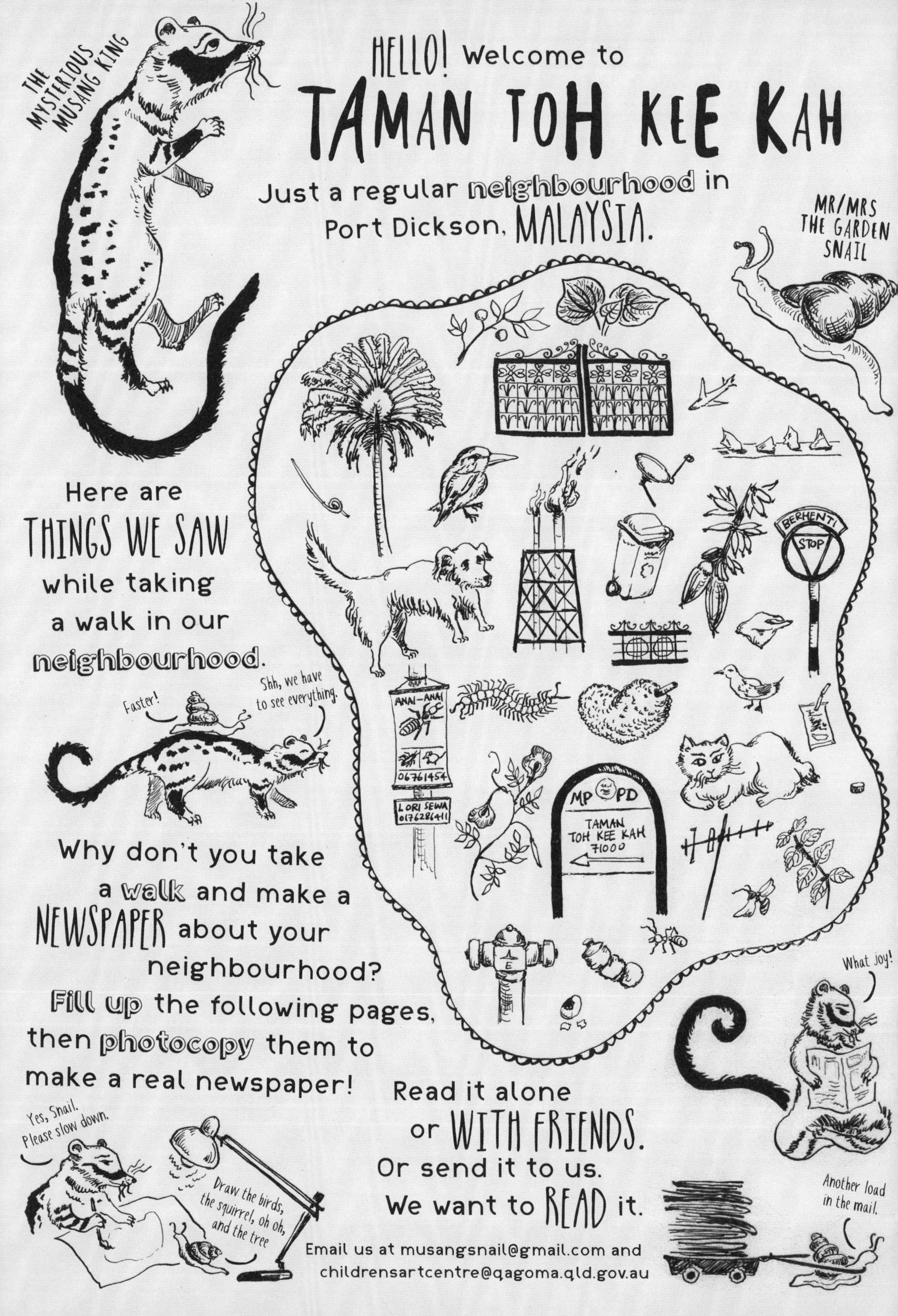
THE MYSTERIOUS MUSANG KING
HELLO! Welcome to
TAMAN TOH KEE KAH
Just a regular neighbourhood in Port Dickson, MALAYSIA.
MR/MRS THE GARDEN SNAIL
BERHENTI
STOP
ANAI-ANAI
06761454
LORI SEWA
0176286411
MP PD
TAMAN TOH KEE KAH 71000
E
Here are THINGS WE SAW while taking a walk in our neighbourhood.
Faster!
Shh, we have to see everything.
Why don't you take a walk and make a NEWSPAPER about your neighbourhood?
Fill up the following pages, then photocopy them to make a real newspaper!
Read it alone or WITH FRIENDS.
Or send it to us.
We want to READ it.
What joy!
Yes, Snail. Please slow down.
Draw the birds, the squirrel, oh oh, and the tree
Another load in the mail.
Email us at musangsnail@gmail.com and childrensartcentre@qagoma.qld.gov.au

What's the name of YOUR 'hood? Write it here BIG!
Find out the meaning/history of the name.

What price is your paper? Or is it FREE?

Day Month Year

M T W T F S S

Circle the day

Circle the weather

TOTALLY REGULAR NEIGHBOURHOOD DIGEST

Trace the dotted lines to build a border

Draw what you saw, heard or smelled.

SNIFF

Use up the whole space.

LOCAL 'HOOD IS WEIRD AND AMAZING

by ______________
your name

Was it a fine day for a walk? Legs and eyeballs alive, yes, it was! I've lived here since what year? ________

Speaking of eyeballs, here's some stuff I saw on my walk:

1.
2.
3.

Luckily, my ears reported for duty too, so I heard:

1.
2.
3.

And my nose! It wants to tell you what it smelled:

1
2.
3.

That's not all. As I was walking, I felt (circle all that apply): hot • sad • shy • tired • happy • bored • friendly • silly • sweaty • wheeee! • lonely • hungry • worried • weird • scared • cold • itchy • quiet • naughty • peaceful • lalalala • angry • chatty • hopeful • puzzled. Other feelings?

____

LEAF OF THE DAY

Pick up a leaf and paste it here

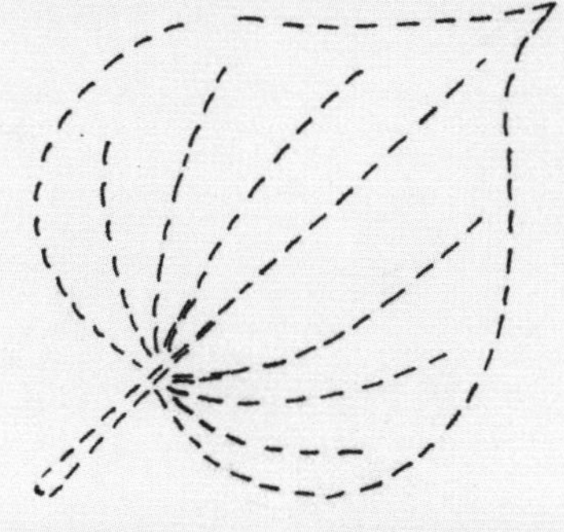

Think about shops or services you might want and create ads for them. Anything is possible. You could make an ad for a neighbourhood circus that doesn't exist yet. Ask shopkeepers and others if they would like you to make them an ad for this paper. It could be free, or you could charge money for it.

advertisement

advertisement

advertisement

advertisement

ASIA FUN PARK

FREE ENTRANCE

GETTIN' HOME

Draw a simple map of your neighbourhood. Start with your house in the centre.

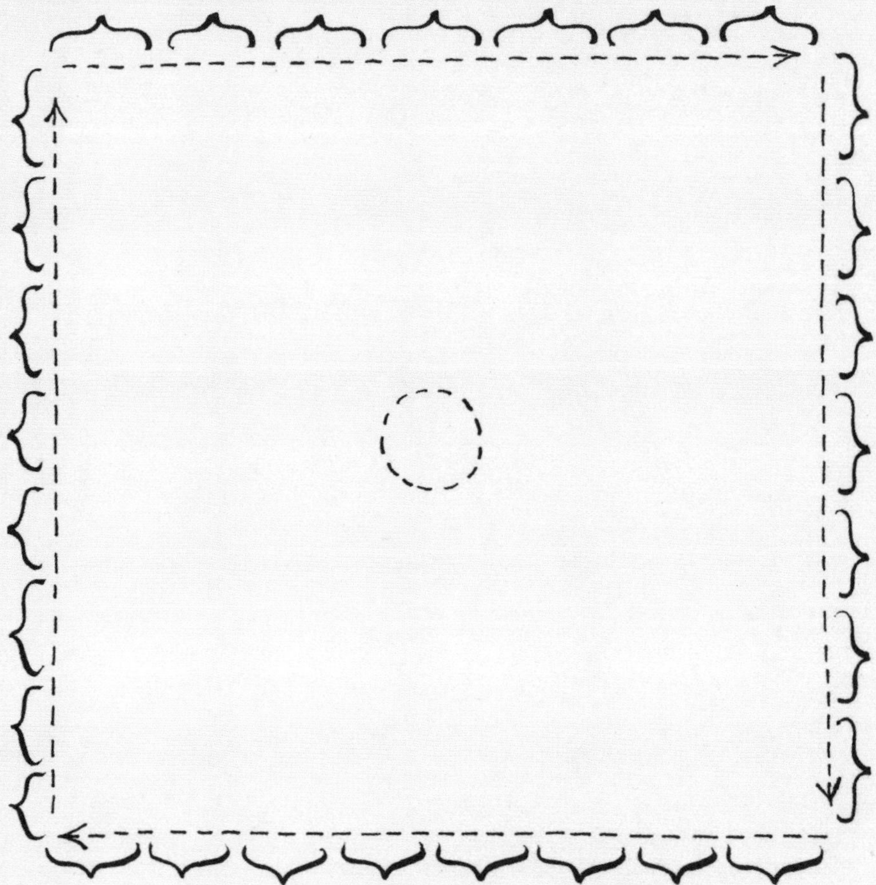

GUESS THE PLACE

Describe a place on your map. Can someone guess what it is from your description? Write the correct answer upside down at the bottom of the page.

Answer:

PERSON OF THE DAY

Someone from your 'hood

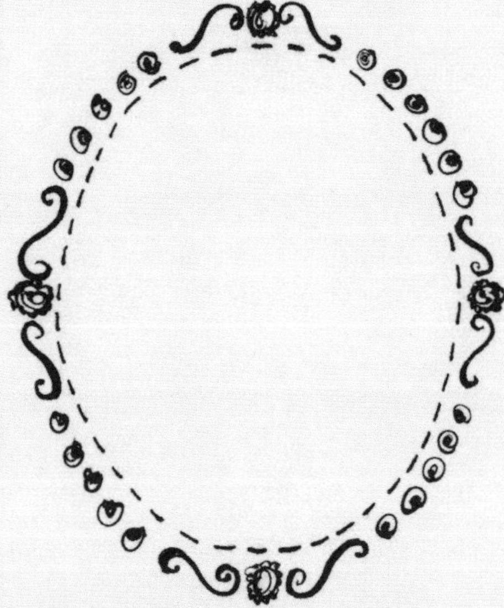

Draw their portrait

Ask them their:

Name:

Age:

LET'S HEAR FROM THE WEEDS

Look for plants growing wild out of cracks or on the footpath. Look down at the grass. Draw a row of different weeds for the Mysterious Musang King to hide behind.

DIRT OF THE DAY

Rub some dirt here (wash your hands afterwards)

DOING TIME WITH A TREE

How does one hang out with a tree? These steps show you how:

1. Find a tree. Bonus if it is on the map you drew on Page 28.
2. Stand close to your tree and count from 1 to 10 sloooooowly.
3. Walk around your tree, then skip around it.
4. Touch any part of your tree lightly with your fingers, once, twice, three times.
5. Give your tree a name:

   ____

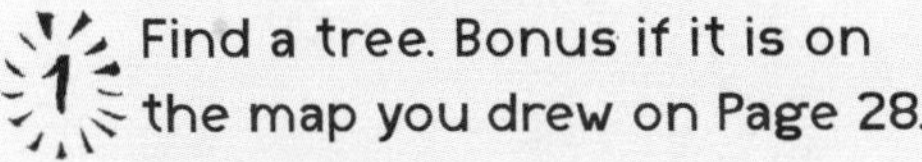

6. Sing any song you know, or have made up, to the tree. Sing it quietly or out loud. What was the song?

   ____

7. Perform a dance for your tree.
8. Write the tree a letter, perhaps adding a drawing to it. Don't forget to sign your name.

RUBBISH ENCOUNTERS

Record the rubbish you see

TYPE OF RUBBISH	HOW MANY
(Example) Plastic Bottle	3

TYPE OF RUBBISH	HOW MANY

COMICS AND FUNNIES

Colour the parts with dots. What do you get?

CONFETTI

Cut and paste tiny bits of coloured paper here, or colour the drawing above. Or do both.

Q	K	K	P	I	N	U	L	J
N	E	E	R	G	A	P	Q	Y
R	Z	F	S	R	H	R	E	T
B	O	E	A	E	B	L	C	E
V	A	Y	M	Y	L	O	U	D
J	L	G	H	O	D	L	M	G
C	X	F	W	N	B	W	E	I

Search for the words that name the colours of these things: leaf, sky, road, lemon. Circle the words with their colour.

Answers: See page 76

Make a character...

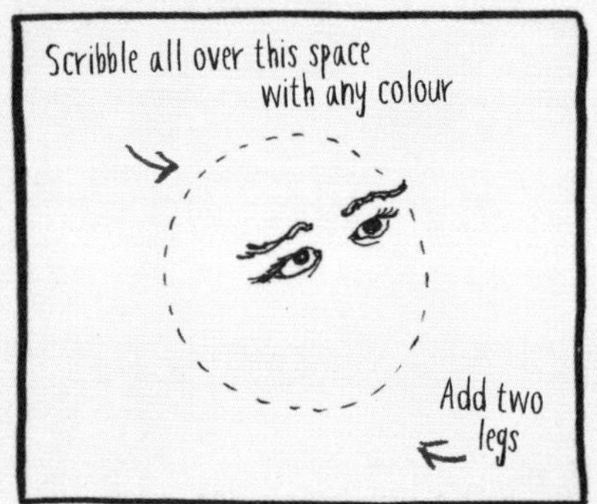

Name: ___________

Make them a friend...

Name: ___________

"CROWN"

STARRING: The Mysterious Musang King

END

"GOLD"

STARRING: Mr/Mrs. the Snail

Delicious durian fruit with bright yellow flesh

END

Excellent. Your characters want to be in a comic and only you can help them! Are you ready to make a comic?

END

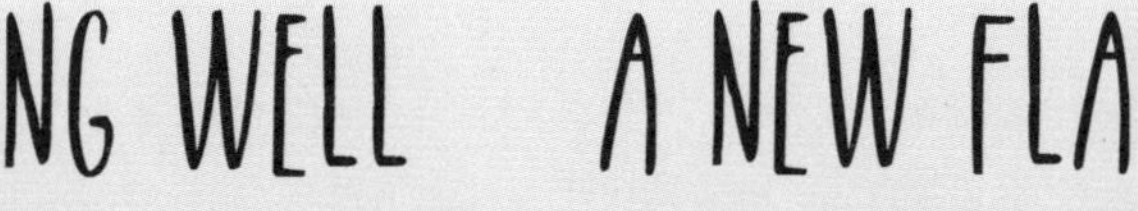

WISHING WELL

How could your neighbourhood be better? Collect suggestions from the people in your 'hood and list them here. Illustrate these ideas.

A NEW FLAG

Design a flag to represent your neighbourhood! Remember the drawings you made on Page 27. Why not use some of them here?

ABOUT

Write about yourself and this newspaper.

This activity newspaper was created by Sharon Chin. Feel free to reproduce for non-commercial purposes, with credit, please.
Thank you to the team at APT8 Kids. Thank you Mothers News and Lynda Barry for their inspiring work. Visit: www.sharonchin.com

THE THREE OF US live in a city and have surrounded ourselves with AMUSING THINGS including people, PETS and other animals, objects of all kinds, a library of BOOKS and films, and a garden.

RAMIN HAERIZADEH, ROKNI HAERIZADEH, & HESAM RAHMANIAN

Iran/United Arab Emirates

In SUCH a place, almost anything can be INSPIRING; from the movement of a grasshopper to a mouse caught by the house cat, to a DRAWING or a film by an artist.

Night of Captiva 2014
Courtesy: The artists

THE COLOUR OF EACH DAY

Every day of the week, we wear a DIFFERENT COLOUR.
Then we note the objects we find that are the colour of each day.

These colours, which can be found in traditional Islamic architecture, are based on the legend of BAHRAM GUR, the Sasanian King who ordered his architect to construct seven domes for each of his princesses. The colour of each dome is said to represent the seven DIFFERENT PLANETS the princesses came from:

Saturday is BLACK for Saturn, Sunday is YELLOW for the Sun.
Monday is GREEN for the Moon, Tuesday is RED for Mars, Wednesday is BLUE for Mercury,
Thursday is TAN for Jupiter and Friday is WHITE for Venus.

You might like to try wearing the colour of the day as you complete the activities!

MONDAY

GREEN IS THE COLOUR OF GARDENS, THE PERFECT PLACE TO PLAY.

Collect THREE GREEN ITEMS from nature and then stick them here or use them to make a picture.

TUESDAY

RED IS THE COLOUR OF FIRE, WHICH IS VERY HOT AND DRY.

Name a few items that are HOT, then draw them here.

WEDNESDAY

BLUE IS THE COLOUR OF THE SKY. LOOK UP AND SEE WHAT YOU FIND.

Do you see the sun, clouds or birds? DRAW what you can see.

THURSDAY

TAN IS THE COLOUR OF SOIL, WHERE THINGS CAN GROW.

Draw what is growing in your
favourite place in the GARDEN.

FRIDAY

WHITE IS THE COLOUR OF LIGHT, WHICH HELPS YOU TO SEE
AND MAKES EVERYTHING CLEAR.

Fill up this space with LEAD PENCIL
and use your eraser to make a picture.

SATURDAY

BLACK IS THE COLOUR OF WISDOM,
JUST LIKE THE DARK NIGHT THAT LETS YOU SEE THE MOON.

Draw your friend's EYES
in as much detail as possible.

SUNDAY

YELLOW IS THE COLOUR OF THE SUN,
SO IT'S THE BEST DAY TO BE JOYFUL.

What flower do you associate with the SUN?
Draw it here.

What I LOVE about where I live
is my small home and workshop
facing the SEA and the
mountains behind me.

NICOLAS MOLÉ

France/New Caledonia

My favourite thing about
being an ARTIST is
the FREEDOM it gives me.

My WORK is a mix of
several techniques. It's a
combination of the traditional
and the CONTEMPORARY.

Self-portrait 2006
Courtesy: The artist

Nicolas Molé and Mariana Molteni
Hnalapa (coté mur) (detail) 2013
Collection: FACKO

Pages 40-41
Sunset (detail) 2013
Courtesy: The artist

CAN YOU FIND THE BIRD?

How many EYES are hiding in the SHRUBBERY?

Answer: See page 77

COLOUR IN the drawing.

THE GUARDIAN'S ROOM

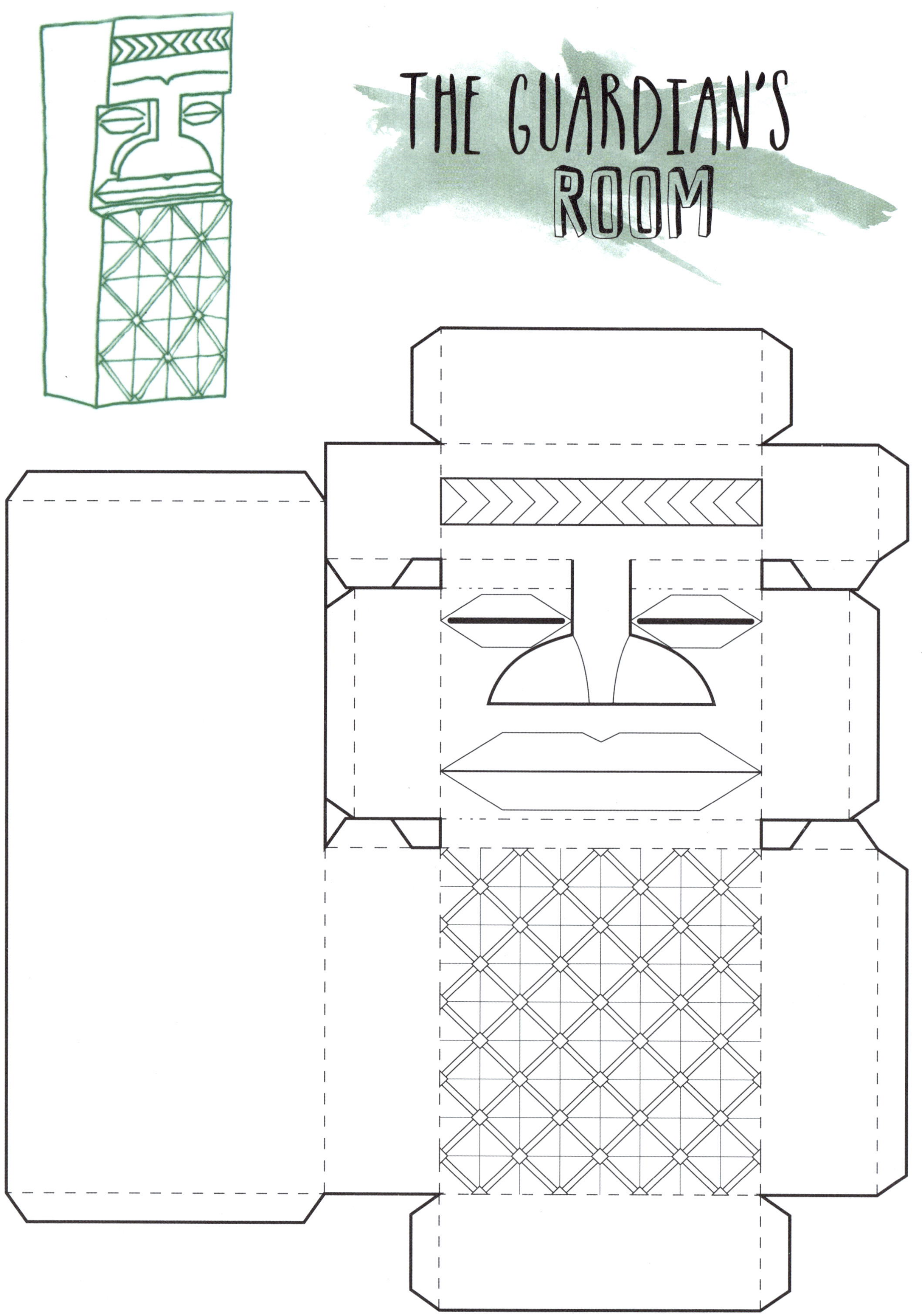

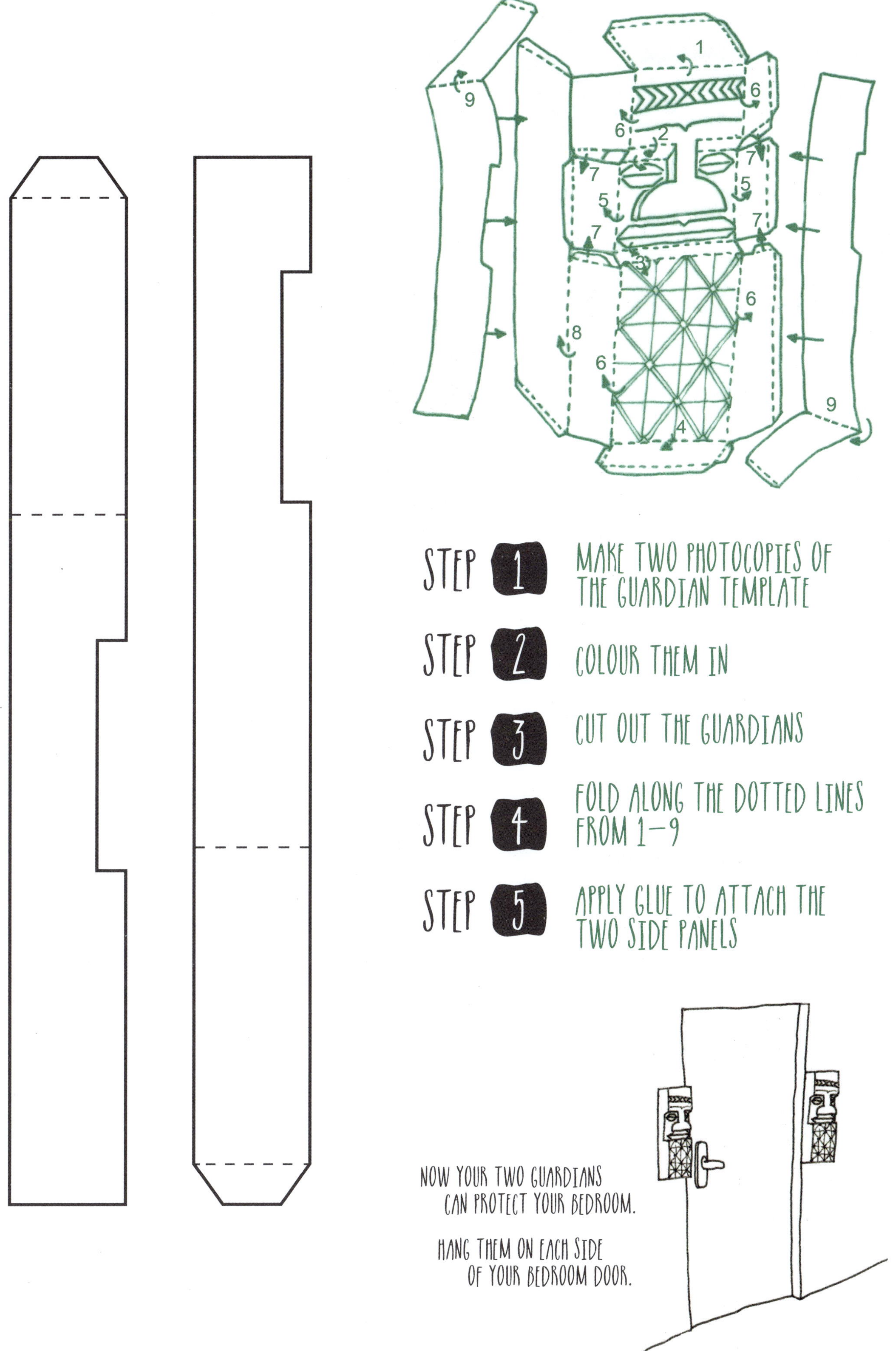
STEP 1
MAKE TWO PHOTOCOPIES OF THE GUARDIAN TEMPLATE
STEP 2
COLOUR THEM IN
STEP 3
CUT OUT THE GUARDIANS
STEP 4
FOLD ALONG THE DOTTED LINES FROM 1–9
STEP 5
APPLY GLUE TO ATTACH THE TWO SIDE PANELS
NOW YOUR TWO GUARDIANS CAN PROTECT YOUR BEDROOM.
HANG THEM ON EACH SIDE OF YOUR BEDROOM DOOR.

YELENA: I studied PAINTING and I like the way THICK oil paint lies on the canvas. I like seeing the NUANCES of colour.

VIKTOR: My FAVOURITE material to work with is graphite as it has so many POSSIBILITIES.

In our artworks we try to show the UNUSUAL side of ordinary things. Showing things from a different perspective helps us to UNDERSTAND the world.

YELENA VOROBYEVA & VIKTOR VOROBYEV

Kazakhstan

We are inspired to create artwork by the different patterns we see in REAL LIFE. Ordinary household objects harbour a LOT of secrets.

From 'Necessary Additions. Home Archive' series 2010
Courtesy: The artists

Our ARTWORK series

'NECESSARY ADDITIONS. HOME ARCHIVE'

is about looking DIFFERENTLY at the past, to get to KNOW it, and to 'work' with it.

We suggest you look into your FAMILY HISTORY as a research project and use it to make ART.

1. Find some photographs of your mum or dad as a baby or, better still, your grandparents.
2. Ask your parent or grandparent what they were called when they were young and what they liked.
3. Consider the photographs carefully – what are they wearing, what toys or other things do they have?
4. How are the items in the old photographs different from things you have now? What do you have in common?
5. Scan or photocopy your photographs and print them out on a sheet of paper. Glue them on the pages provided making sure you leave plenty of white space around them.
6. Look at each photograph. Is there anything in them that prompts your imagination? What can you draw, glue or write to change it? Add some new elements and see how you have changed their world!

From 'Necessary Additions. Home Archive' series 2010
Courtesy: The artists

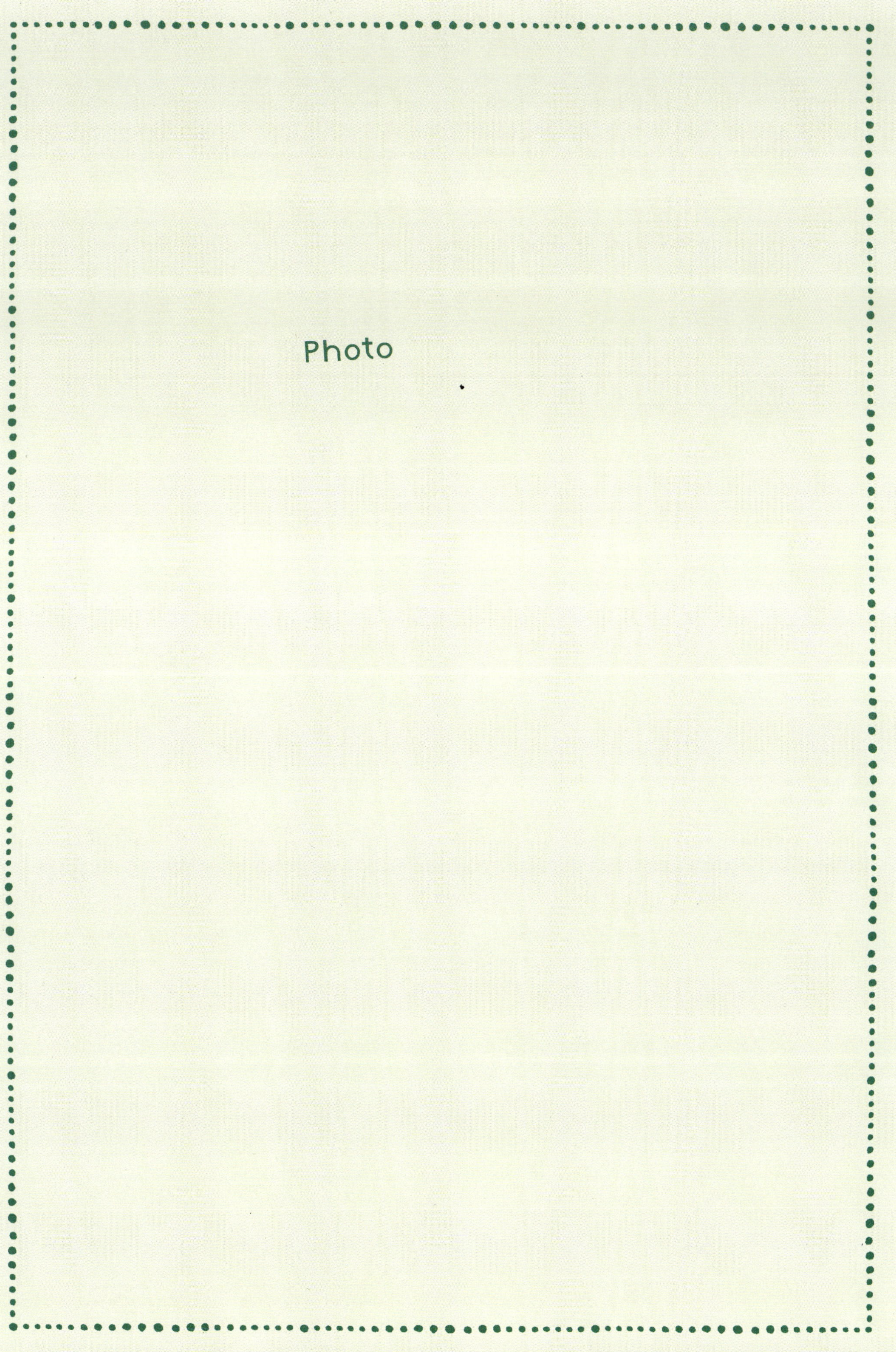
Photo

Photo

Photo

My ART is about human rights. I am a BIG fan of equality for all. I'd like to see equality for women and land rights for aboriginal people all around the WORLD. I am also interested in the IMPACT of people on the environment. My work is about self-respect and respect for others.

RICHARD BELL

Australia

My FAVOURITE thing to do as an artist is to PAINT. I LOVE painting. I love the mess I can make and creating something that looks GOOD.

Richard Bell and Emory Douglas
We Can Be Heroes 2014
Collection: Art Gallery of New South Wales

Tell a story or EXPRESS a message about the environment by colouring in the PICTURES and filling in the speech bubbles for the characters in each SCENE.

SILVANA: My favourite thing about being an ARTIST is to have the opportunity to INVENT and play with ideas.

GABRIELLA MANGANO & SILVANA MANGANO

Australia

GABRIELLA: I LOVE the collaboration process and SHARING a creative space with Silvana.

Visual Structures (still) 2014
Courtesy: Anna Schwartz Gallery and the artists

We are INTERESTED in movement in our work and we do this through the use of drawing, body compositions and sound.

Drawing repetitive lines with TWO coloured pens can create interesting and unexpected results.

In these activities you can create MOVEMENT on the paper and discover how LINES can seem to build sculptural forms.

Choose your TWO FAVOURITE felt pen colours. Hold them together. COPY the line above until you reach the bottom. See if the line CHANGES.

Select a GREEN and a PINK felt pen. Hold them together.
BEGIN a small circle in the middle of the page and draw AROUND and AROUND until you cover the whole page.

Select an ORANGE and a BLUE felt pen. Hold them together.
Starting at the left side, see how many VERTICAL LINES
you can draw on the page.

Select a PURPLE and a PINK felt pen. Hold them together. Draw a small square in the middle of the page and make it BIGGER and BIGGER until you cover the whole page.

Once you have finished, cut the pages along the dotted line and flip them to MIX AND MATCH the shapes and colours.

Select a BLUE and a GREEN felt pen. **Hold them together**. Starting at the left side, see how many HORIZONTAL LINES you can DRAW on the page.

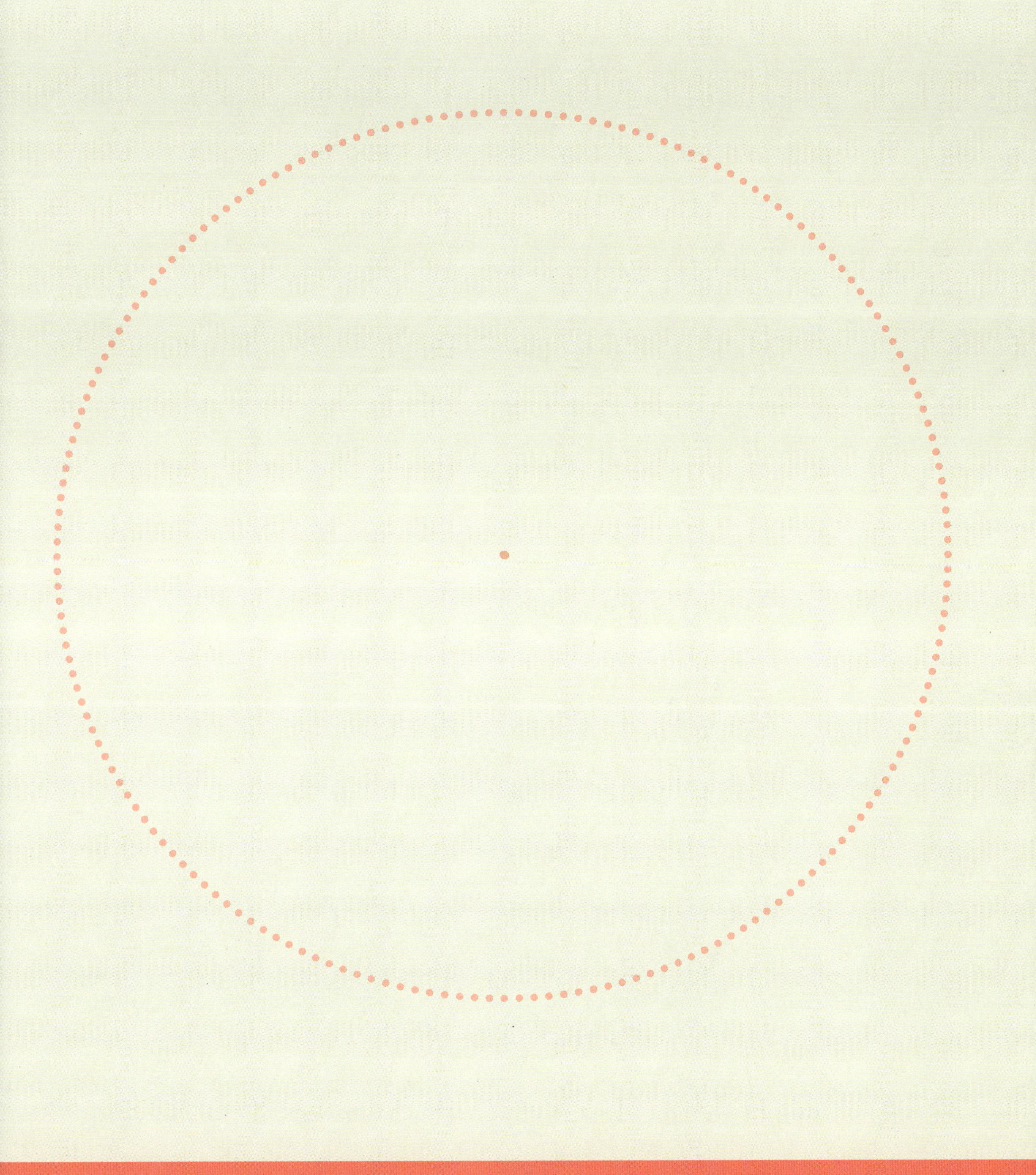

Choose your TWO FAVOURITE felt pen colours. **Hold them together**. Starting at the **middle point**, draw straight lines out to the EDGE of the circle. As you draw MORE and MORE lines the circle will begin to FILL with colour.

My favourite thing about being an ARTIST is creating new things that could only be born in my IMAGINATION.

GERELKHUU GANBOLD

Mongolia

I think that people are very INTERESTING. Their activities, desires and INFLUENCES ON OUR WORLD inspire me to create artworks.

I am interested in the history of MY COUNTRY and its traditions. In my opinion, WHERE I CAME FROM and where I am going define me.

Self-portrait 2015
Courtesy: The artist

Red horses (detail) 2013
Courtesy: The artist

In Mongolia, MONGOL ZURAG is a style of painting characterised by fine brushwork, BRIGHT colours and THEMES from everyday life.

I have drawn this lion using this STYLE.

In the following pages you can see how I have TRANSFORMED the lion into a ROBOT.

How to draw A LION ROBOT

Step 1

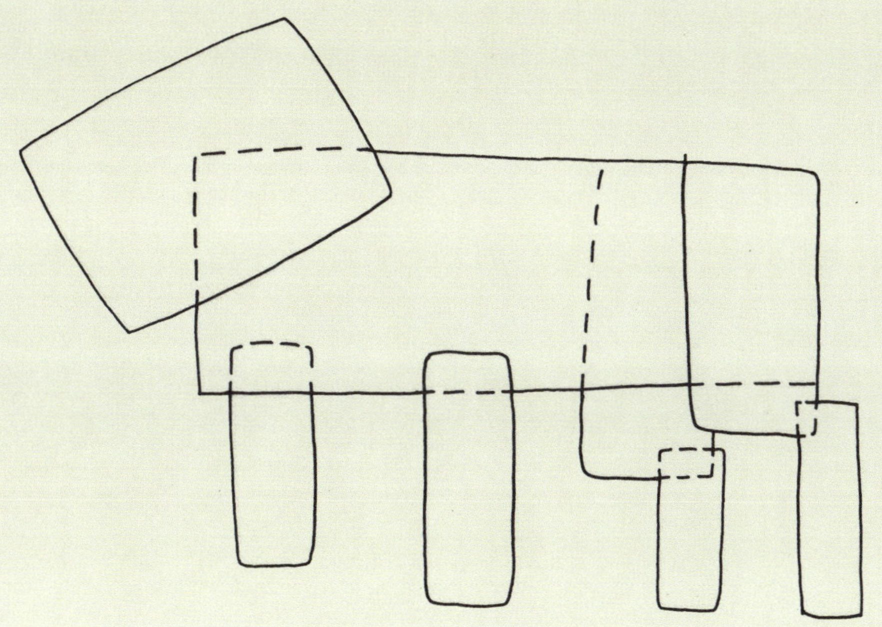

LIGHTLY DRAW SQUARE AND RECTANGULAR SHAPES ON THE PAGE SO THAT SOME CAN BE ERASED IN THE NEXT STEP.

Step 2

DRAW THE LION'S EYES, NOSE AND MOUTH. DRAW ANOTHER RECTANGLE FOR THE MANE AND ADD MORE SHAPE TO THE LEGS AND BODY. ERASE ANY LINES THAT OVERLAP.

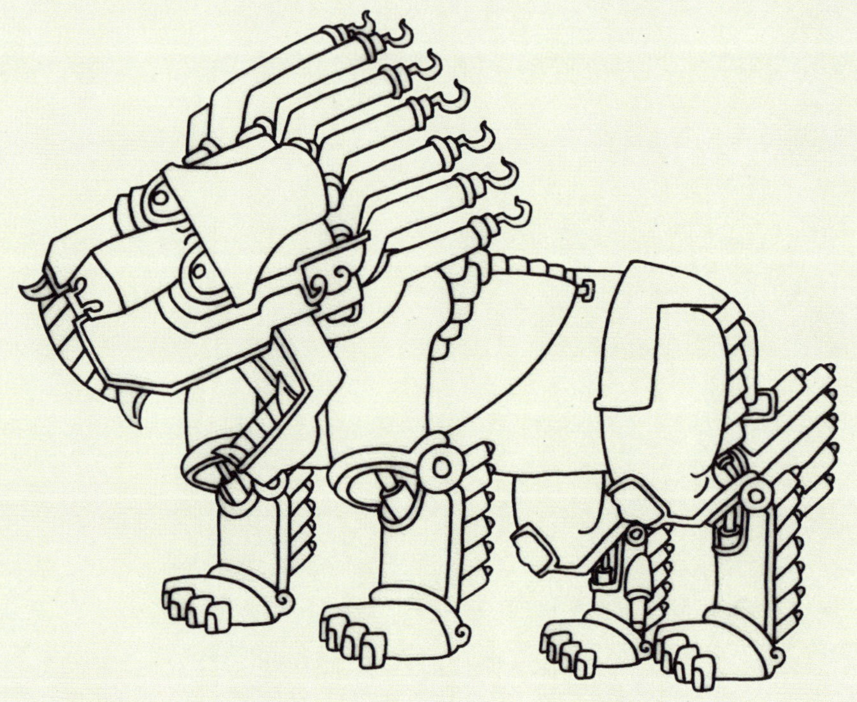

DRAW ALL THE SMALL DETAILS, INCLUDING THE PUPILS IN THE EYES, NOSTRILS, MANE, TEETH AND CLAWS. EVEN THOUGH THIS IS A LION ROBOT, IT SHOULD LOOK ALIVE! ADD WRINKLES BETWEEN THE EYES AND MUSCLES ALONG THE LEGS.

Step 4

NOW YOUR LION ROBOT IS READY TO BE COLOURED IN. CHOOSE YOUR COLOURS CAREFULLY AND THINK ABOUT WHAT MIGHT WORK WELL TOGETHER. IN MY DRAWING, I CHOSE BROWN, BLUE AND GREEN BUT YOU CAN CHOOSE ANY COLOURS YOU LIKE.

YOU CAN ALSO ADD MORE DETAIL TO YOUR DRAWING USING SHADING AND PATTERNS.

Now it's YOUR turn ...

Konstantine Kitiashvili

Natalia Vatsadze

Vladimer Khartishvili

Teimuraz Kartlelishvili

Ekaterine Ketsbaia

Zurab Kikvadze

We are SIX ARTISTS who work together in a group called Bouillon.

We were born in different cities in different years.

The oldest is Natalia – she is the wisest; the youngest is Vladimer – he is the most STUBBORN; Ekaterine DRESSES very well; Zurab loves to think; Teimuraz loves to grumble; and we all LOVE Konstantine, he is the FAVOURITE of the group.

BOUILLON GROUP

Georgia

The artworks we CREATE are inspired by life. Our FAVOURITE materials to work with are ideas.

SUPRA 2014
Courtesy: The artists

BOUILLON SOUP

BOUILLON IS A BROTH, AND A FRENCH TERM MEANING 'TO BOIL'.
IT IS MADE BY SIMMERING MEAT, FISH OR VEGETABLES IN WATER WITH HERBS.

JUST LIKE BOUILLON SOUP, WHICH IS MADE FROM DIFFERENT INGREDIENTS, OUR GROUP IS MADE UP OF DIFFERENT PEOPLE WORKING TOGETHER, AND OUR ART IS ABOUT LOTS OF DIFFERENT IDEAS.
WE MADE THE BOUILLON SOUP AND INVITED GUESTS TO SHARE OUR MEAL.

NOW WE INVITE YOU TO MAKE OUR SOUP FOR SHARING WITH YOUR FAMILY AND FRIENDS.
MAKE SURE YOU HAVE AN ADULT HELP YOU IN THE KITCHEN.

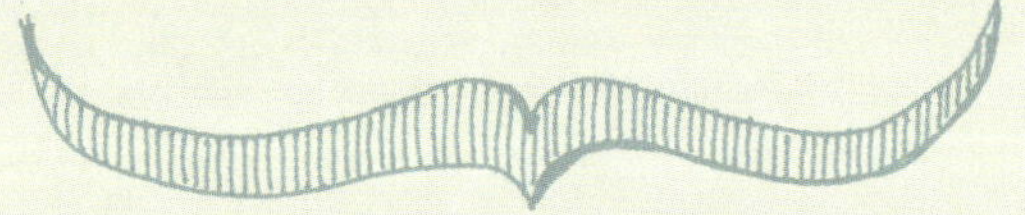

INGREDIENTS

1 chicken or 750g chicken pieces (on the bone)
2 carrots, sliced
8 cups of water
1 handful of coriander, finely chopped
Pinch of black pepper
Salt to taste

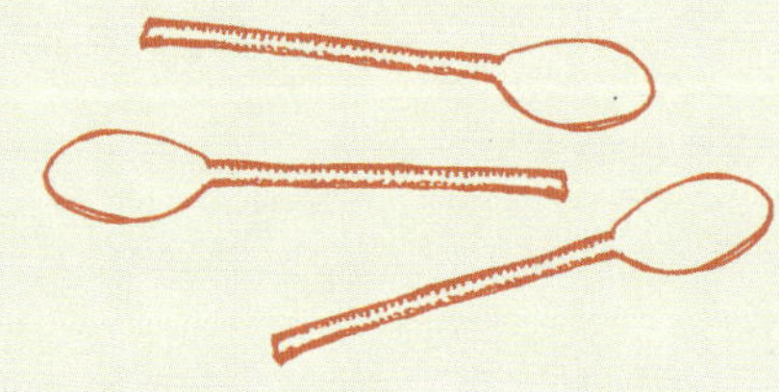

INSTRUCTIONS

1. Put all ingredients together in a pot and bring to the boil. Skim the froth.
2. Simmer for 1 hour, or until the chicken is cooked.
3. Remove the chicken from the pot and shred meat.
4. Return the shredded meat to the pot and add seasoning (salt and pepper) to taste.
5. Invite your guests to share your meal and the performance is complete!

WHAT IS YOUR FAVOURITE MEAL?

DRAW IT HERE.

It takes LOTS of different ingredients to create a GREAT MEAL. DRAW your ingredients here.

Think about WHO you would invite to SHARE this meal.
Now draw a PICTURE of them.

Angela Tiatia

Aotearoa New Zealand/Australia b.1973

Page 8
Self-portrait 2015
Collage
42 x 29.5cm
Courtesy: The artist and Alcaston Gallery, Melbourne

Page 9
Heels (from 'An Inventory of Gestures' series) (still) 2014
Single-channel HD video, 16:9, 1:50 minutes (looped), colour, sound, ed. 1/8
Purchased 2015. Queensland Art Gallery | Gallery of Modern Art Foundation
Collection: Queensland Art Gallery
Courtesy: The artist and Alcaston Gallery, Melbourne

Sharon Chin

Malaysia b.1980

Page 24
Self-portrait in Fire (火), Earth (土), Metal (金), Water (水) and Wood (木) 2015
Chinese ink on paper
21 x 29.7cm
Courtesy: The artist

Page 25
Mandi Bunga/Flower Bath 2013
Collaborative public performance
Dimensions variable
Commissioned for Singapore Biennale 2013
Courtesy: The artist
Photograph: Yee I-Lann

Answers from page 30: green, blue, grey, yellow

Pushpa Kumari

India b.1969

Page 16
Myself in Madhubani Style 2015
Material ink on paper
21 x 29.7cm
Courtesy: The artist

Page 17
Prem jalkida (The intoxication of love and attraction) 2015
Ink on acid free paper
61 x 46cm (approx.)
Proposed for the Queensland Art Gallery Collection

Ramin Haerizadeh

Iran b.1975

Rokni Haerizadeh

Iran b.1978

Hesam Rahmanian

USA b.1980

Page 32
Ramin Haerizadeh, Rokni Haerizadeh and Hesam Rahmanian
Photograph © Laurie Lambrecht 2014
Courtesy: The artists

Page 33
Night of Captiva 2014
Mixed media on paper
155 x 375cm
Courtesy: The artists

Nicolas Molé

France/New Caledonia b.1975

Page 38
Self-portrait 2006
Digital drawing
Dimensions variable
Courtesy: The artist

Page 39
Nicolas Molé (aka Le Singe Vert) and
Mariana Molteni / Argentina/New Caledonia b.1975
Hnalapa (coté mur) (detail) 2013
Site-specific audio-visual installation commissioned for 'Ma maison est un jardin', Centre Culturel Tjibaou, Noumea
Dimensions variable
Collection: FACKO

Page 40-41
Sunset (detail) 2013
Digital collage, pen ink and digital print
21 x 29.7cm
Courtesy: The artist

Answer from page 41: 3 eyes

Yelena Vorobyeva

Turkmenistan b.1959

Viktor Vorobyev

Kazakhstan b.1959

Page 44
Personal photography kindly supplied by the artists.

Page 45
From 'Necessary Additions. Home Archive' series 2010
Digital prints, ink, whitewash and pencil on grey paper
42 x 29.7cm
Courtesy: The artists

Page 46
From 'Necessary Additions. Home Archive' series 2010
Digital prints, ink, whitewash and pencil on grey paper
29.7 x 21cm
Courtesy: The artists

From 'Necessary Additions. Home Archive' series 2010
Digital prints, ink, whitewash and pencil on grey paper
42 x 29.7cm
Courtesy: The artists

Richard Bell

Australia b.1953
Kamilaroi/Jiman/Kooma people

Page 50
Artist Richard Bell participating in a children's workshop for APT8 Kids activity *15 Minutes*, Brisbane, July 2015
Photograph: Mark Sherwood

Page 51
Richard Bell and
Emory Douglas / United States b.1943
We Can Be Heroes 2014
Acrylic on linen
180 x 240cm
Collection: Art Gallery of New South Wales

Gabriella Mangano

Australia b.1972

Silvana Mangano

Australia b.1972

Page 56
Personal photography kindly supplied by the artists.

Page 57
Visual Structures (still) 2014
Six-channel video, time variable, black and white, sound
Courtesy: Anna Schwartz Gallery and the artists

Gerelkhuu Ganbold

Mongolia b.1988

Page 64
Self-portrait 2015
Ink on paper
12 x 10cm
Courtesy: The artist

Page 65
Red horses (detail) 2013
Watercolour on paper
364 x 124cm
Courtesy: The artist

Bouillon Group

Georgia est. 2008

Page 70
Personal photography kindly supplied by the artists.

Page 71
SUPRA 2014
Photograph of video performance
Performance in Stockholm, at IASPIS, the Swedish Arts Grants Committee's international programme for visual artists and designers
Courtesy: The artists

CHILDREN'S
ART CENTRE

THE QUEENSLAND ART GALLERY | GALLERY OF MODERN ART'S CHILDREN'S ART CENTRE IS A LEADER IN DEVELOPING ART ACTIVITIES AND PROGRAMMING FOR CHILDREN.

THE CHILDREN'S ART CENTRE FOCUSES ON INTERACTIVE PROJECTS FOR YOUNG VISITORS, ENABLING CHILDREN AND FAMILIES TO EXPERIENCE THE MANY WAYS ARTISTS APPROACH THEIR WORK. ITS AWARD-WINNING PUBLICATIONS FOR CHILDREN INCLUDE:

PATTERN POWER: BLENDING IN AND STANDING OUT

In collaboration with Jemima Wyman, 2014

Honourable Mention in the International Design Awards 2014, in the Print: Books category.

Finalist in the international REVERE awards 2015, in the Beyond the Classroom category.

Shortlisted in the Museums Australia Multimedia and Publication Design Awards (MAPDA) 2015, in the Children's Book (Level B) category.

LET'S CREATE AN EXHIBITION WITH A BOY NAMED CAI

by Cai Guo-Qiang, 2013

Honourable Mention in the International Design Awards 2013, in the Print: Books category.

Finalist in the international REVERE awards 2014, in the Beyond the Classroom category.

THE SACRED HILL

by Gordon Hookey, 2013

HAHAN AND FRIENDS

In collaboration with Uji Handoko Eko Saputro (aka Hahan), 2012

Winner in the Museums Australia Multimedia and Publication Design Awards (MAPDA) 2013, in the Education Material (Level C) category.

Honourable Mention in the international American Association of Museums (AAM) Publications Design Competition 2013, in the Books category.

PORTRAIT OF SPAIN FOR KIDS

2012

Awarded a silver medal in the International Design Awards 2012, in the Print: Books category.

Awarded a bronze medal in the international Moonbeam Children's Book Awards 2012, in the Book Arts category.

Awarded first place in the international Association of Education Publishers Distinguished Achievement Award 2013, in the category Supplemental Resources: The Arts.

Shortlisted in the Children's Book Council of Australia Awards (CBCA) 2013, Eve Pownall Award for Information Books.

DRAWING LIFE FOR KIDS: MY ART JOURNAL

2012

Joint Winner in the Museums Australia Multimedia and Publication Design Awards (MAPDA) 2012, in the Education Material (Level C) category.

Awarded a gold medal in the international Independent Publisher Book Awards (IPPY Awards) 2013, in the Children's Interactive category.

Awarded Best Designed Children's Non-Fiction Book and Best Designed Children's Cover of the Year in the Australia Publishers Association's 60th Annual Book Design Awards.

SURREALISM FOR KIDS

2011

Winner in in the Museums Australia Multimedia and Publication Design Awards (MAPDA) 2012, in the Book (Level C) category.

Awarded a bronze medal in the international Independent Publisher Book Awards (IPPY Awards) 2012, in the Children's Interactive category.

Shortlisted in the Children's Book Council of Australia Awards (CBCA) 2012, Eve Pownall Award for Information Books.

21ST CENTURY ART FOR KIDS

2010

Honourable mention in the international American Association of Museums (AAM) Design Awards 2011, in the Education Resources category.

PUBLISHER

Queensland Art Gallery | Gallery of Modern Art
Stanley Place, South Bank, Brisbane
PO Box 3686, South Brisbane
Queensland 4101 Australia
qagoma.qld.gov.au

A Queensland Art Gallery | Gallery of Modern Art
Children's Art Centre publication
qagoma.qld.gov.au/kids

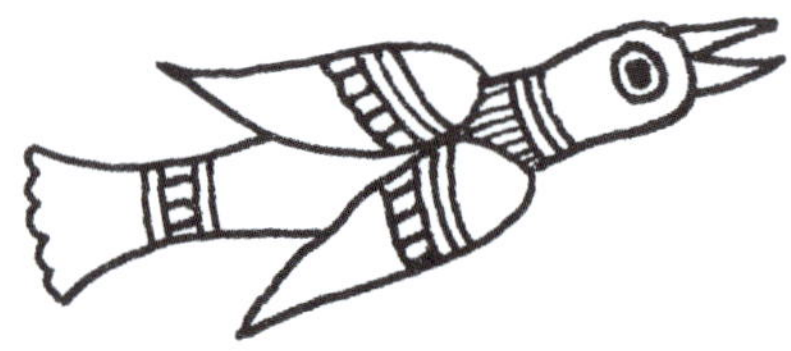

A CiP for this publication is available from the National Library of Australia.
ISBN: 9781921503788

Published in conjunction with APT8 Kids, held in association with 'The 8th Asia Pacific Triennial of Contemporary Art', an exhibition organised by and held at the Queensland Art Gallery | Gallery of Modern Art, Brisbane, Australia, 21 November 2015 – 10 April 2016.

'The Asia Pacific Triennial of Contemporary Art' (APT) is the Queensland Art Gallery | Gallery of Modern Art's flagship contemporary art exhibition series. Since 1993, the APT series has driven the Gallery's focus on the region and enabled the development of one of the world's most significant collections of contemporary Asian and Pacific art.

THANKS

The Gallery would like to thank the 'APT8 Kids' artists who collaborated with the Children's Art Centre to create this book, and the children who participated in trials for the publication's activities. Thank you also to Lucinda Wolber for research assistance.

Draw, Make, Create publication concept, development, design and editing

Simon Wright, Assistant Director, Learning and Public Engagement
Tamsin Cull, Head of Public Engagement
Laura Mudge, A/Senior Program Officer, Children's Art Centre
Michael O'Sullivan, Design Manager
Stella Danalis, A/Senior Graphic Designer
Christina Pagliaro, Senior Editor
Stephanie Kennard, Assistant Editor
Jacqueline Tunny, Public Programs Officer, Children's Art Centre
Samantha Relihan, Public Programs Officer, Children's Art Centre
Aaron Seeto, Curatorial Manager of Asian and Pacific Art
Ruth McDougall, Curator, Pacific Art
Kyla McFarlane, Curator, Australian Art
Tarun Nagesh, Associate Curator, Asian and Pacific Art
Ellie Buttrose, Associate Curator, International Contemporary Art

Typeset in Flama, Shababa and Supernova. Printed by Australian Book Connection, China.

The Gallery gratefully acknowledges the Tim Fairfax Family Foundation for making the *Draw, Make, Create* publication possible.

APT8 KIDS PRINCIPAL BENEFACTOR

The illustrations on this page were produced by Pushpa Kumari for her activity in *Draw, Make, Create*.